Read This... ™ On Your Birthday

A GUIDED JOURNAL
CELEBRATING A CHILD'S LIFE
BIRTH TO 21

By Christy Howard & Annie Presley

Special thanks to our friends who provided inspiration and personal stories along the way:

Wanda Chinnery · Steve DiGiacinto · Melinda Garcia
Mary Heausler · Escher Holloway · Sommer Howard
Wendy Jensen · Amy Lee · Ann O'Meara

Cover and book design:
Frank M. Addington

Read This…™ On Your Birthday
By Christy Howard & Annie Presley

First Edition

Printed in the United States of America

ISBN: 978-0-9883425-3-8

www.BooksByAce.com

Other books in the series include:
Read This…™ When I'm Dead
Read This…™ On Our Anniversary

ACE Publishing LLC
KANSAS CITY, MO

Welcome to the Story of a Loved Child

This book helps you capture the amazing early years of a beloved child. Help them remember their childhood stories, the very best of who they are and what they have mastered. Engage them to remember some of the fantastic events in their early years. Remind them about the accomplishments they have made. Inspire them to believe they truly have much to offer.

Celebrate each birthday by creating a history the child will cherish in the years to come! Throughout this book Christy and Annie share their thoughts, experiences and ideas about what mattered to them in childhood and what made meaningful, positive impacts on children they have watched grow up.

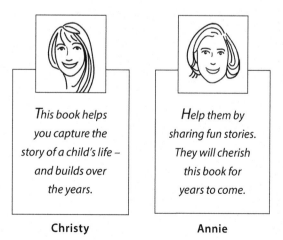

This book helps you capture the story of a child's life – and builds over the years.

Christy

Help them by sharing fun stories. They will cherish this book for years to come.

Annie

This Book is About a Loved Child

Filled out for:

_____

NAME

Filled out by:

_____

NAME

_____

RELATIONSHIP TO THE CHILD

CONTENTS

A note from Christy:

When our daughter, Sommer, was very young – maybe not even born yet – a friend told me about letters his children received on Christmas morning listing accomplishments and milestones from that year. My husband and I adopted that tradition and there was always a letter by Sommer's stocking filled with her best accomplishments that year — from helping someone cross the street to overcoming a difficult situation to mastering something new — like a "real" dive into the pool.

Helping children remember happy moments and accomplishments lifts their spirits, and is a wonderful way for adults to chronicle unique experiences and memories. Later it reminds them of all the love they have enjoyed.

What a joy it is to look back and see all the accomplishments in a child's life!

A note from Annie:

As children, my brother, sister and I remember celebrating our birthdays. Yet we lack the details of any specific ones because our mom died when we were kids and no one recorded our special times. As adults we would love to have some written stories of celebrations, school year milestones and those happy carefree days.

This book is designed to guide you through commemorating a child's birth to 21st birthdays. On the momentous 21st birthday, you make final entries and give the child the book – the story of their early years.

Happy Birthday

Feliz Cumpleaños

Bon Anniversaire

Alles Gute Zum Geburtstag

生日快乐

Lá Breithe Shona Duit

Buon Compleanno

Grattis På Födelsedagen

Okazji Urodzin

สุขสันต์วันเกิด

Gratulerer Med Dagen

One

About The Day You Were Born

and

When We First Met

"As soon as I saw you, I knew an adventure was going to happen."

Winnie-the-Pooh to Piglet

Winnie-the-Pooh

A.A. Milne

About The Day You Were Born

You were born at (time) _____

on (day of the week) _____

(date) _____

in (location) _____

The weather was:

You were named by _____

on _____ (date).

I was born during a blizzard and have heard the story so many times I can almost feel the cold and see the snow.

Your name was chosen because:

How I learned you were born:

When We First Met

We first met on _____ (date)

when I _____

This describes our first moments together

Did you go to visit or were you there at birth? Did you fly or drive? If you first met days or years after the child was born, describe that timing!

I nicknamed my niece "The Peanut" because at under 5 pounds she fit easily into my two hands and was no bigger than a peanut.

This describes how I felt when I met you

Your first few days…

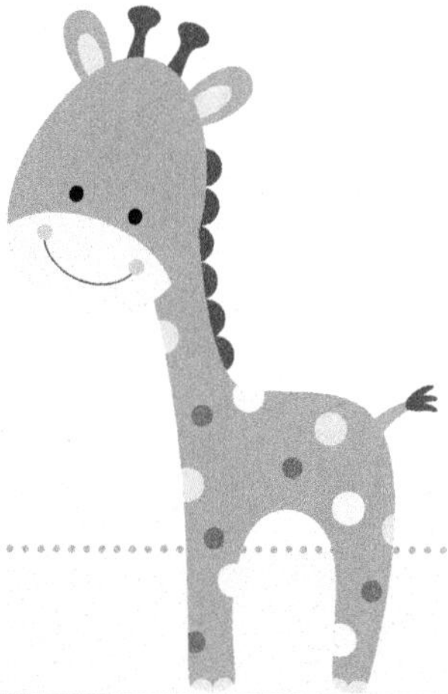

"'Sometimes,' said Pooh, 'the smallest things take up the most room in your heart.'"

Winnie-the-Pooh

A.A. Milne

CHAPTER

Two

Your Baby and Toddler Years

YOUR FIRST BIRTHDAY

YOUR SECOND BIRTHDAY

YOUR THIRD BIRTHDAY

Your **First** Birthday

A Description of the Celebration

The People Who Celebrated with You
(list family and friends)

Your **First** Birthday

About You This Year

You Learned

You Mastered

You Improved

*Don't forget
favorite animals –
real or stuffed!*

You Overcame

You Loved

Your **First** Birthday

More About You This Year

Where you lived and with whom

How you spent your days

Your spiritual activities

Your favorite foods

Your favorite songs/books/movies

Favorite activities/games/toys/classes

My favorite thing to watch you do was

What makes this baby laugh? Our daughter first laughed watching her mobile circle around. We couldn't stop watching her laugh and still talk about that day.

Your **First** Birthday

My Note to You About This Year

What super cute things does this baby do?

Your **First** Birthday

A Footprint or Hand-Print of the Birthday Boy or Girl

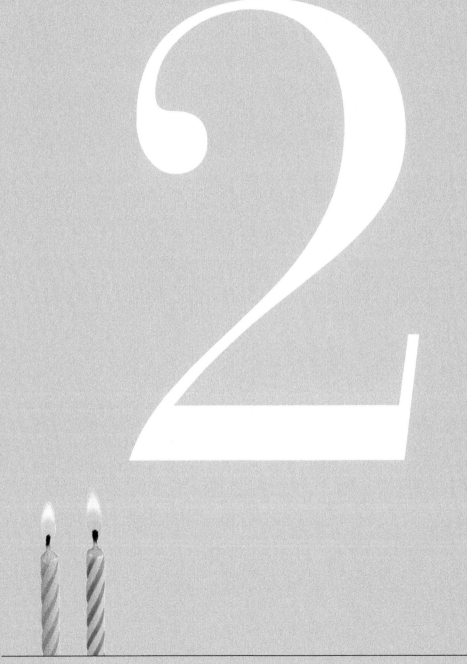

22

Your **Second** Birthday

A Description of the Celebration

The People Who Celebrated with You
(list family and friends)

Your **Second** Birthday

About You This Year

You Learned

You Mastered

You Improved

You Overcame

Be sure to mention friends!

You Loved

You Helped

Your **Second** Birthday

More About You This Year

Where you lived and with whom

How you spent your days

Your triumphs

Your spiritual activities

Holiday traditions you loved

Notable events this year (popular and in the news)

Your **Second** Birthday

Favorite Things

Your hero(es)

Your favorite foods

Your favorite songs/books/movies

Your favorite activities/games/toys/classes

Your favorite things to learn

My favorite thing to watch you do was

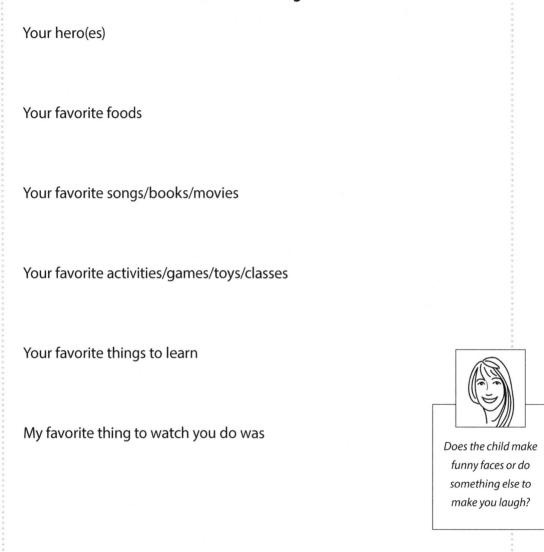

Does the child make funny faces or do something else to make you laugh?

Your **Second** Birthday

My Note to You About This Year

A drawing by the birthday boy or girl

This yellow area is for the child to express themselves.

I want to be a _____ when I grow up

Birthday Signature

Your **Third** Birthday

A Description of the Celebration

The People Who Celebrated with You
(list family and friends)

Your **Third** Birthday

About You This Year

You Learned

You Mastered

You Improved

You Overcame

Any favorite physical or musical accomplishments?

You Loved

You Helped

Your **Third** Birthday

More About You This Year

Where you lived and with whom

How you spent your days

Your triumphs

Your spiritual activities

Holiday traditions you loved

Notable events this year (popular and in the news)

Your **Third** Birthday

Favorite Things

Your hero(es)

Your favorite foods

Your favorite songs/books/movies

Has the child "found themselves" in any messy situations... makeup, food, toothpaste...?

Your favorite activities/games/toys/classes

Your favorite things to learn

My favorite thing to watch you do was

Your **Third** Birthday

My Note to You About This Year

A drawing by the birthday boy or girl

This yellow area is for the child to express themselves.

I want to be a _____ when I grow up

Birthday Signature

"Today you are You, That is truer than true. There is no one alive Who is Youer than You."

Happy Birthday to You

Dr. Seuss

CHAPTER
Three

As A Young Child

BIRTHDAYS 4 — 8

Your **Fourth** Birthday

A Description of the Celebration

The People Who Celebrated with You
(list family and friends)

Your **Fourth** Birthday

About You This Year

You Learned

You Mastered

You Improved

You Overcame

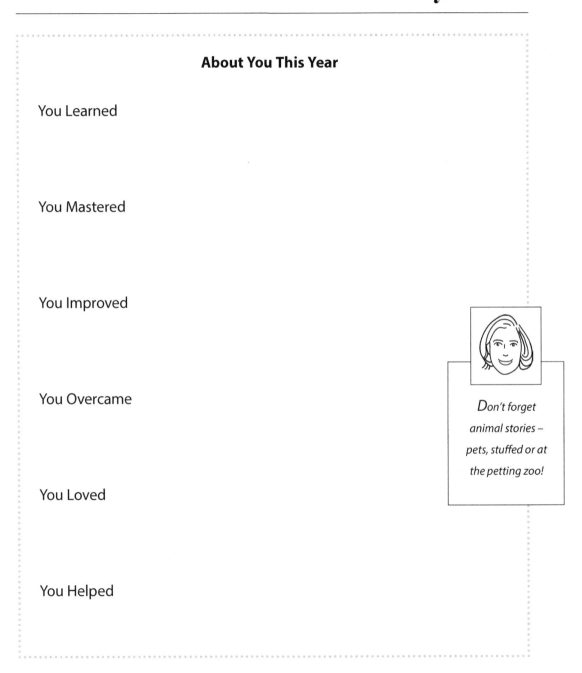

Don't forget animal stories – pets, stuffed or at the petting zoo!

You Loved

You Helped

Your **Fourth** Birthday

More About You This Year

Where you lived and with whom

How you spent your days (school and non-school time)

Your triumphs

Your spiritual activities

Holiday traditions you loved

Notable events this year (popular and in the news)

From the child's perspective

Next year I want to…

Your **Fourth** Birthday

Favorite Things

Your hero(es)

Your favorite foods

Your favorite songs/books/movies

Your favorite activities/games/toys/classes

Your favorite things to learn

My favorite thing to watch you do was

Be sure to describe any favorite dress-up outfits, favorite toys or stuffed animal "friend".

Your **Fourth** Birthday

My Note to You About This Year

A drawing by the birthday boy or girl

*This yellow area
is for the child to
express themselves.*

I want to be a _____ when I grow up

Birthday Signature

Your **Fifth** Birthday

A Description of the Celebration

My daughter loved her treasure hunt party. I wrote clues on Hello Kitty note paper and the kids raced to find and read each clue until they found the prize.

The People Who Celebrated with You
(list family and friends)

Your **Fifth** Birthday

About You This Year

You Learned

You Mastered

You Improved

You Overcame

You Loved

Be sure to mention friends!

You Helped

Your **Fifth** Birthday

More About You This Year

Where you lived and with whom

How you spent your days (school and non-school time)

Your triumphs

Your spiritual activities

Holiday traditions you loved

Notable events this year (popular and in the news)

From the child's perspective

Next year I want to…

Your **Fifth** Birthday

Favorite Things

Your hero(es)

Your favorite foods

Your favorite songs/books/movies

Your favorite activities/games/toys/classes

Your favorite things to learn

My favorite thing to watch you do was

Describe some favorite stories the child likes to hear. Are there any favorite parts of the story?

Your **Fifth** Birthday

My Note to You About This Year

This yellow area is for the child to express themselves.

A drawing by the birthday boy or girl

I want to be a _____ when I grow up

Birthday Signature

Your **Sixth** Birthday

A Description of the Celebration

My husband's favorite birthday party activity was spontaneous – the boys ran outside to play with toy trucks in a rain storm!

The People Who Celebrated with You
(list family and friends)

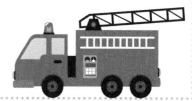

Your **Sixth** Birthday

About You This Year

You Learned

You Mastered

You Improved

You Overcame

Any favorite clubs, sports or teams?

You Loved

You Helped

Your **Sixth** Birthday

More About You This Year

Where you lived and with whom

How you spent your days (school and non-school time)

Your triumphs

What activities are most fun now? Maybe something like riding a bike, dancing, reading, playing a particular game, cooking, cleaning…?

Your spiritual activities

Holiday traditions you loved

Notable events this year (popular and in the news)

From the child's perspective

Next year I want to…

Your **Sixth** Birthday

Favorite Things

Your hero(es)

Your favorite foods

Your favorite songs/books/movies

Your favorite activities/games/toys/classes

Your favorite things to learn

My favorite thing to watch you do was

Your **Sixth** Birthday

My Note to You About This Year

A drawing by the birthday boy or girl

This yellow area is for the child to express themselves.

I want to be a _____ when I grow up

Birthday Signature

Your **Seventh** Birthday

A Description of the Celebration

The People Who Celebrated with You
(list family and friends)

Your **Seventh** Birthday

About You This Year

You Learned

You Mastered

You Improved

You Overcame

Write about any special animals – pets or otherwise.

You Loved

You Helped

Your **Seventh** Birthday

More About You This Year

Where you lived and with whom

How you spent your days (school and non-school time)

Your triumphs

Your spiritual activities

Holiday traditions you loved

Notable events this year (popular and in the news)

From the child's perspective

Next year I want to…

Your **Seventh** Birthday

Favorite Things

Your hero(es)

Your favorite foods

Your favorite songs/books/movies

Your favorite activities/games/toys/classes

What are some favorite daily clothes? – T-shirts, jeans, suits, hats, dresses, special socks?

Your favorite things to learn

My favorite thing to watch you do was

Your **Seventh** Birthday

My Note to You About This Year

A drawing by the birthday boy or girl

This yellow area is for the child to express themselves.

I want to be a _____ when I grow up

Birthday Signature

Your **Eighth** Birthday

A Description of the Celebration

The People Who Celebrated with You
(list family and friends)

Your **Eighth** Birthday

About You This Year

You Learned

You Mastered

You Improved

You Overcame

Be sure to mention friends.

You Loved

You Helped

Your **Eighth** Birthday

More About You This Year

Where you lived and with whom

How you spent your days (school and non-school time)

Your triumphs

Your spiritual activities

Holiday traditions you loved

Notable events this year (popular and in the news)

From the child's perspective

Next year I want to…

Your **Eighth** Birthday

Favorite Things

Your hero(es)

Your favorite foods

Your favorite songs/books/movies

Our family loved to invite family friends to play board games and domino games. I can still hear the laughter.

Your favorite activities/games/toys/classes

Your favorite things to learn

My favorite thing to watch you do was

Your **Eighth** Birthday

My Note to You About This Year

A drawing by the birthday boy or girl

This yellow area is for the child to express themselves.

I want to be a _____ when I grow up

Birthday Signature

"Laughter is timeless, Imagination has no age, and Dreams are forever."

Walt Disney

CHAPTER

Four

Your Adolescent Years

BIRTHDAYS 9 — 12

Your **Ninth** Birthday

A Description of the Celebration

The People Who Celebrated with You
(list family and friends)

Your **Ninth** Birthday

About You This Year

You Learned

You Mastered

You Improved

You Overcame

*A*ny favorite clubs,
sports or teams?

You Loved

You Helped

Your **Ninth** Birthday

More About You This Year

Where you lived and with whom

How you spent your days (school and non-school time)

Your triumphs

Your spiritual activities

Holiday traditions you loved

Notable events this year (popular and in the news)

From the child's perspective

Next year I want to…

Your **Ninth** Birthday

Favorite Things

Your hero(es)

Your favorite foods

Your favorite songs/books/movies

Describe his/her haircut this year.

Your favorite activities/games/toys/classes

Your favorite things to learn

My favorite thing to watch you do was

Your **Ninth** Birthday

My Note to You About This Year

A drawing by the birthday boy or girl

This yellow area is for the child to express themselves.

I want to be a _____ when I grow up

Birthday Signature

Your **Tenth** Birthday

A Description of the Celebration

The People Who Celebrated with You
(list family and friends)

Your **Tenth** Birthday

About You This Year

You Learned

You Mastered

You Improved

You Overcame

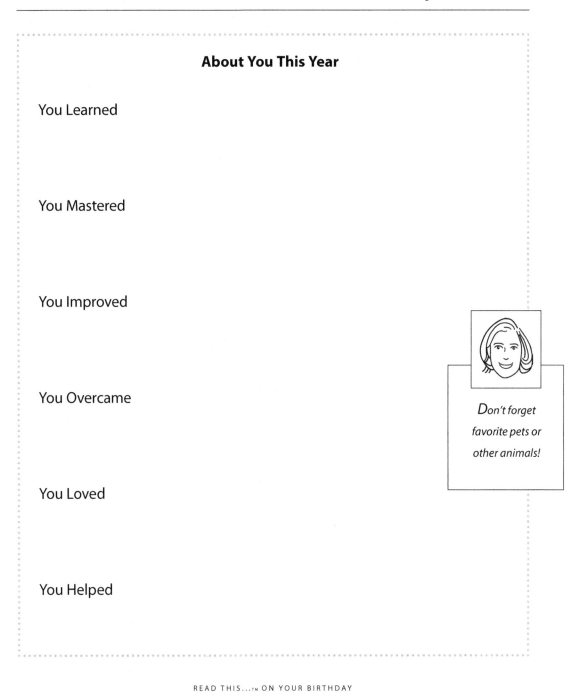

Don't forget favorite pets or other animals!

You Loved

You Helped

Your **Tenth** Birthday

More About You This Year

Where you lived and with whom

How you spent your days (school and non-school time)

Your triumphs

Your spiritual activities

After school I would ride the red wagon down the hill with my younger cousins. We drove with the wagon handle. That hill seemed huge. Now it looks like a gentle slope!

Holiday traditions you loved

Notable events this year (popular and in the news)

From the child's perspective

Next year I want to…

Your **Tenth** Birthday

Favorite Things

Your hero(es)

Your favorite foods

Your favorite songs/books/movies

Your favorite activities/games/toys/classes

Your favorite things to learn

My favorite thing to watch you do was

Your **Tenth** Birthday

My Note to You About This Year

*This yellow area
is for the child to
express themselves.*

A drawing by the birthday boy or girl

I want to be a _____ when I grow up

Birthday Signature

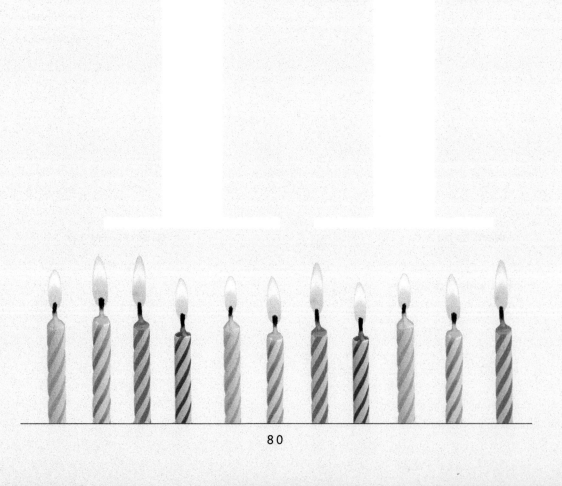

Your **Eleventh** Birthday

A Description of the Celebration

The People Who Celebrated with You
(list family and friends)

Your **Eleventh** Birthday

About You This Year

You Learned

You Mastered

You Improved

You Overcame

Be sure to mention friends!

You Loved

You Helped

Your **Eleventh** Birthday

More About You This Year

Where you lived and with whom

How you spent your days (school and non-school time)

Your triumphs

Your spiritual activities

Holiday traditions you loved

Notable events this year (popular and in the news)

From the child's perspective

Next year I want to…

Your **Eleventh** Birthday

Favorite Things

Your hero(es)

Your favorite foods

Your favorite songs/books/movies

Your favorite activities/games/toys/classes

Your favorite things to learn

My favorite thing to watch you do was

What favorite movies came out this year?

Your **Eleventh** Birthday

My Note to You About This Year

A drawing by the birthday boy or girl

This yellow area is for the child to express themselves.

I want to be a _____ when I grow up

Birthday Signature

Your **Twelfth** Birthday

A Description of the Celebration

The People Who Celebrated with You
(list family and friends)

Your **Twelfth** Birthday

About You This Year

You Learned

You Mastered

You Improved

You Overcame

In the 6th grade, on my 12th birthday, some buddies and I started a rock band. We were the last act in the school talent show so we called ourselves "The Grand Finale."

You Loved

You Helped

Your **Twelfth** Birthday

More About You This Year

Where you lived and with whom

How you spent your days (school and non-school time)

Your triumphs

Your spiritual activities

Holiday traditions you loved

Notable events this year (popular and in the news)

From the child's perspective

Next year I want to…

Your **Twelfth** Birthday

Favorite Things

Your hero(es)

Are there some favorite school activities now?

Your favorite foods

Your favorite songs/books/movies

Your favorite activities/games/toys/classes

Your favorite things to learn

My favorite thing to watch you do was

Your **Twelfth** Birthday

My Note to You About This Year

A drawing by the birthday boy or girl

This yellow area is for the child to express themselves.

I want to be a _____ when I grow up

Birthday Signature

"*Promise me you'll always remember: You're BRAVER than you believe, STRONGER than you seem, and SMARTER than you think.*"

Christopher Robin to Winnie-the-Pooh

Winnie-the-Pooh

A.A. Milne

CHAPTER

Five

Your Early Teen Years

BIRTHDAYS 13 — 15

94

Your **Thirteenth** Birthday

A Description of the Celebration

The People Who Celebrated with You
(list family and friends)

Your **Thirteenth** Birthday

About You This Year

You Learned

You Mastered

You Improved

You Overcame

You Loved

Any favorite clubs, sports or teams?

You Helped

Your **Thirteenth** Birthday

More About You This Year

Where you lived and with whom

How you spent your days (school and non-school time)

Your triumphs

Are clothing styles changing? Describe how they have changed for the child.

Your spiritual activities

Holiday traditions you loved

Notable events this year (popular and in the news)

Your **Thirteenth** Birthday

Favorite Things

Your hero(es)

Your favorite foods

Your favorite songs/books/movies

Your favorite activities/games/toys/classes

Your favorite things to learn

My favorite thing to watch you do was

Your **Thirteenth** Birthday

My Note to You About This Year

This yellow area is for the teen to share their thoughts.

I improved or overcame

When I'm not in school I _____
(Do you work, play sports, volunteer, make music, read, write…
and do you like it?)

I'm thinking of becoming a(n) _____
when I grow up.

My goals for next year are

Your **Fourteenth** Birthday

A Description of the Celebration

The People Who Celebrated with You
(list family and friends)

Your **Fourteenth** Birthday

About You This Year

You Learned

You Mastered

You Improved

Don't forget favorite pets or animals.

You Overcame

You Loved

You Helped

Your **Fourteenth** Birthday

More About You This Year

Where you lived and with whom

How you spent your days (school and non-school time)

Your triumphs

Your spiritual activities

Holiday traditions you loved

Notable events this year (popular and in the news)

Your **Fourteenth** Birthday

Favorite Things

Your hero(es)

Your favorite foods

Your favorite songs/books/movies

Who does this child look up to? – Either a person in their life or someone they have read about or seen on TV.

Your favorite activities/games/toys/classes

Your favorite things to learn

My favorite thing to watch you do was

Your **Fourteenth** Birthday

My Note to You About This Year

This yellow area is for the teen to share their thoughts.

I improved or overcame

When I'm not in school I _____
(Do you work, play sports, volunteer, make music, read, write…
and do you like it?)

I'm thinking of becoming a(n) _____
when I grow up.

My goals for next year are

Your **Fifteenth** Birthday

A Description of the Celebration

The People Who Celebrated with You
(list family and friends)

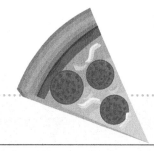

Your **Fifteenth** Birthday

About You This Year

You Learned

You Mastered

You Improved

You Overcame

*A*ny fun friend
stories?

You Loved

You Helped

Your **Fifteenth** Birthday

More About You This Year

Where you lived and with whom

How you spent your days (school and non-school time)

Your triumphs

Your spiritual activities

Holiday traditions you loved

Notable events this year (popular and in the news)

Your **Fifteenth** Birthday

Favorite Things

Your hero(es)

Your favorite foods

Your favorite songs/books/movies

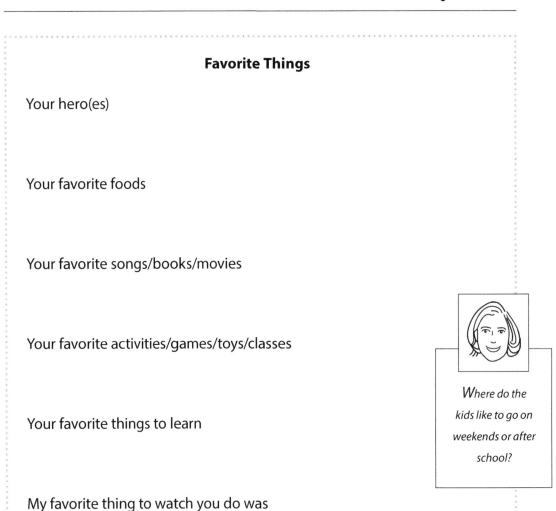

Your favorite activities/games/toys/classes

Where do the kids like to go on weekends or after school?

Your favorite things to learn

My favorite thing to watch you do was

Your **Fifteenth** Birthday

My Note to You About This Year

This yellow area is for the teen to share their thoughts.

I improved or overcame

When I'm not in school I _____
(Do you work, play sports, volunteer, make music, read, write…
and do you like it?)

I'm thinking of becoming a(n) _____
when I grow up.

My goals for next year are

"You have brains in your head.
You have feet in your shoes.
You can steer yourself any
direction you choose.
You're on your own, and you
know what you know.
And you are the one who'll
decide where to go..."

Oh the Places You'll Go

Dr. Seuss

CHAPTER

Six

An Independent Teen

BIRTHDAYS 16 — 19

Your **Sixteenth** Birthday

A Description of the Celebration

The People Who Celebrated with You
(list family and friends)

Your **Sixteenth** Birthday

About You This Year

You Learned

You Mastered

You Improved

You Overcame

Any favorite clubs, sports or teams?

You Loved

You Helped

Your **Sixteenth** Birthday

More About You This Year

Where you lived and with whom

How you spent your days (school and non-school time)

Your triumphs

Your spiritual activities

Holiday traditions you loved

Notable events this year (popular and in the news)

Your **Sixteenth** Birthday

Favorite Things

Your hero(es)

Your favorite foods

*Who drives now –
and where?*

Your favorite songs/books/movies

Your favorite activities/games/toys/classes

Your favorite things to learn

My favorite thing to watch you do was

Your **Sixteenth** Birthday

My Note to You About This Year

This yellow area is for the teen to share their thoughts.

I improved or overcame

When I'm not in school I _____

(Do you work, play sports, volunteer, make music, read, write… and do you like it?)

I'm thinking of becoming a(n) _____ when I grow up.

My goals for next year are

120

Your **Seventeenth** Birthday

A Description of the Celebration

The People Who Celebrated with You
(list family and friends)

Your **Seventeenth** Birthday

About You This Year

You Learned

You Mastered

You Improved

You Overcame

You Loved

You Helped

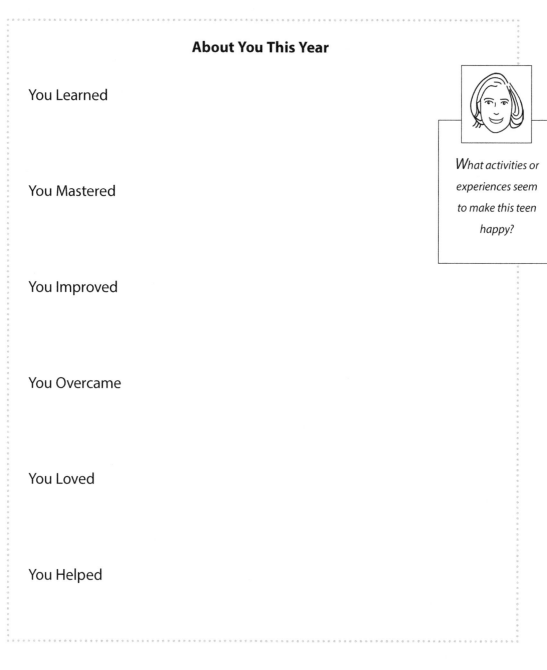

What activities or experiences seem to make this teen happy?

Your **Seventeenth** Birthday

More About You This Year

Where you lived and with whom

How you spent your days (school and non-school time)

Your triumphs

Your spiritual activities

Holiday traditions you loved

Notable events this year (popular and in the news)

Your **Seventeenth** Birthday

Favorite Things

Your hero(es)

Your favorite foods

Your favorite songs/books/movies

Your favorite activities/games/toys/classes

Your favorite things to learn

My favorite thing to watch you do was

Your **Seventeenth** Birthday

My Note to You About This Year

This yellow area is
for the teen to share
their thoughts.

I improved or overcame

When I'm not in school I _____
(Do you work, play sports, volunteer, make music, read, write…
and do you like it?)

I'm thinking of becoming a(n) _____
when I grow up.

My goals for next year are

Your **Eighteenth** Birthday

A Description of the Celebration

The People Who Celebrated with You
(list family and friends)

Your **Eighteenth** Birthday

About You This Year

You Learned

You Mastered

You Improved

Don't forget favorite pets or animals and outdoor adventures.

You Overcame

You Loved

You Helped

Your **Eighteenth** Birthday

More About You This Year

Where you lived and with whom

How you spent your days (school and non-school time)

Your triumphs

Your spiritual activities

Holiday traditions you loved

Notable events this year (popular and in the news)

Your **Eighteenth** Birthday

Favorite Things

Your hero(es)

Your favorite foods

Your favorite songs/books/movies

Your favorite activities/games/toys/classes

Your favorite things to learn

My favorite thing to watch you do was

Your **Eighteenth** Birthday

My Note to You About This Year

This yellow area is for the teen to share their thoughts.

I improved or overcame

When I'm not in school I _____
(Do you work, play sports, volunteer, make music, read, write…
and do you like it?)

I'm thinking of becoming a(n) _____
when I grow up.

My goals for next year are

Your **Nineteenth** Birthday

A Description of the Celebration

My daughter's friends - new and old - gathered at our house to celebrate.

The People Who Celebrated with You
(list family and friends)

Your **Nineteenth** Birthday

About You This Year

You Learned

You Mastered

You Improved

You Overcame

Don't forget friends, pets, clubs and teams.

You Loved

You Helped

Your **Nineteenth** Birthday

More About You This Year

Where you lived and with whom

How you spent your days (school and non-school time)

Your triumphs

Your spiritual activities

Holiday traditions you loved

Notable events this year (popular and in the news)

Your **Nineteenth** Birthday

Favorite Things

Your hero(es)

Your favorite foods

Your favorite songs/books/movies

Your favorite activities/games/toys/classes

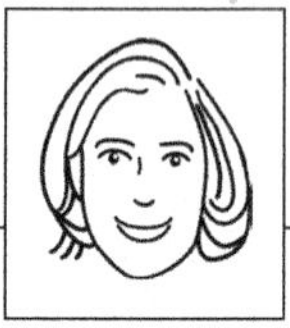

What are some favorite on-the-job experiences?

Your favorite things to learn

My favorite thing to watch you do was

Your **Nineteenth** Birthday

My Note to You About This Year

This yellow area is for the teen to share their thoughts.

I improved or overcame

When I'm not in school I _____
(Do you work, play sports, volunteer, make music, read, write…
and do you like it?)

I'm thinking of becoming a(n) _____
when I grow up.

My goals for next year are

"When I was a boy of fourteen, my father was so ignorant I could hardly stand to have the old man around. But when I got to be twenty-one, I was astonished at how much he had learned in seven years."

Mark Twain

CHAPTER

Seven

Becoming An Adult

BIRTHDAYS 20 — 21

Your **Twentieth** Birthday

A Description of the Celebration

The People Who Celebrated with You
(list family and friends)

Your **Twentieth** Birthday

About You This Year

You Learned

You Mastered

You Improved

You Overcame

You Loved

Be sure to mention, friends, pets, clubs or groups and teams.

You Helped

Your **Twentieth** Birthday

Your **Twentieth** Birthday

Favorite Things

Your hero(es)

Your favorite foods

Your favorite songs/books/movies

Your favorite activities/games/toys/classes

Your favorite things to learn

My favorite thing to watch you do was

Your **Twentieth** Birthday

This yellow area is for the teen to share their thoughts.

I improved or overcame

When I'm not in school I _____
(Do you work, play sports, volunteer, make music, read, write…
and do you like it?)

I'm thinking of becoming a(n) _____
when I grow up.

My goals for next year are

Your **Twenty-first** Birthday

A Description of the Celebration

The People Who Celebrated with You
(list family and friends)

Your **Twenty-first** Birthday

About You This Year

You Learned

You Mastered

You Improved

You Overcame

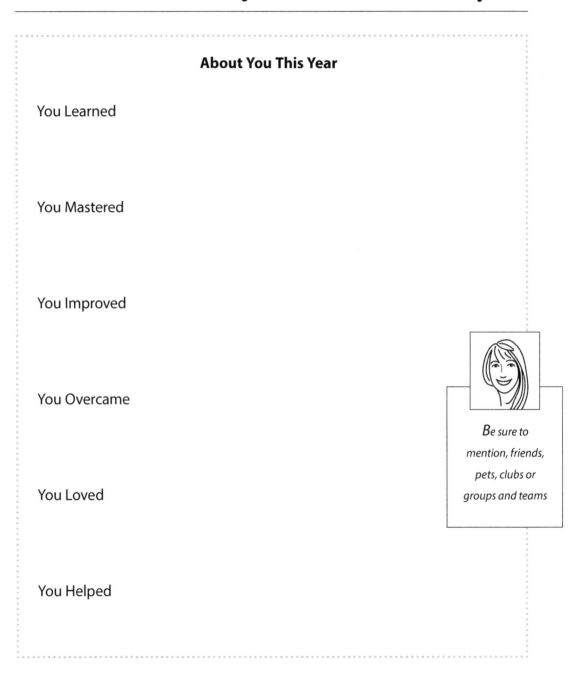

Be sure to mention, friends, pets, clubs or groups and teams

You Loved

You Helped

Your **Twenty-first** Birthday

More About You This Year

Where you lived and with whom

How you spent your days (school and non-school time)

Your triumphs

Your spiritual activities

Holiday traditions you loved

Notable events this year (popular and in the news)

Your **Twenty-first** Birthday

Favorite Things

Your hero(es)

Your favorite foods

Your favorite songs/books/movies

Your favorite activities/games/classes

Your favorite things to learn

My favorite thing to watch you do was

Where would the young lady/man like to live and what would she/he like to be doing in 10 years?

Your **Twenty-first** Birthday

My Goals

In one year I plan to be (working, living, studying…)

In five years I would like to be (working, living, studying…)

In ten years I see my self (working, living, studying…)

A Final Note

**My Note to You About This Year and
My Thoughts and Wishes For You**

Signed _____ Date _____

" 'Why did you do
all this for me?'
Wilber asked.
'I don't deserve it.
I've never done
anything for you.'
'You have been my friend,'
replied Charlotte.
'That in itself is a
tremendous thing.' "

Willber to Charlotte

Charlotte's Web

E. B. White

CPSIA information can be obtained
at www.ICGtesting.com
Printed in the USA
LVOW05*2050171116

513456LV00005B/8/P

9 780988 342538